Standing Beside You

A Book for Bereaved Parents

Linda K. Maurer

Poems reprinted with permission of Bereavement Magazine, 8133 Telegraph Drive, Colorado Springs, Colorado, 80920:

My Photo Album, Jeanne Losey, Shelbyville, Indiana
The Wind In My Arms, JoAnn McMeans, Port Angeles, Washington
The Gift, Joe Lawley, Nuneaton, England

Linda K. Maurer
7386 Buckingham Court
Boulder, CO 80301

ISBN 0-9636977-1-4

Printed by Johnson Printing, Boulder, Colorado

Acknowledgements

My thanks and love to my husband, Larry, for his support and understanding, without which this book would not have been written.

Thanks also to MacDonald King Aston, my editor, and Julie Bettis, who proofread the manuscript.

I would also like to thank my friends Kay Bevington, Kathy Charlton, Gayle Hamer, Reverend John Hess, Kay Massey, Lynn Mullen and Diana Pagano for reviewing my book and encouraging me to complete it for the benefit of all bereaved parents.

Linda Maurer
December 15, 1995
Boulder, Colorado

DEDICATION

This book is dedicated to our daughter,
Molly Marie Maurer, our only child,
who was the joy of our lives
and our best friend.

10/13/71—3/16/91

Table of Contents

Forward i

Introduction iii

Our Story—Our Memories 1

The Shock of Death. 7

Surviving The First Year 11

Mental and Physical Problems. 19

Difficult Situations 23

Your Child's Possessions 29

Marriage 33

Friends 37

The Death of An Only Child. 41

Helping Others 47

Closure. 53

The Spiritual World and Dreams. 57

In Conclusion. 61

Appendix A:
Bereavement Groups 63

Appendix B:
Living Through Grief 71

Forward

Our daughter, Molly Marie, died a violent death in a tragic but preventable accident on March 16, 1991, at the age of nineteen. She was our only child.

The purpose of this book is to give you hope and encouragement for the days, weeks, months, and years ahead of you.

As stated in my first book, I am not a psychiatrist, a psychologist, nor a grief counselor. I am not, by profession, a writer. The advice, suggestions, and ideas given in this book are not professional, but are compiled from my own experiences as a bereaved mother.

Your life is forever changed and dealing with the death of your child will be the greatest challenge of your life.

I sincerely hope the information contained in this book will be of help, comfort, and guidance, in coping with your pain and grief.

God bless you.

Linda K. Maurer

Introduction

In the fall of 1969, my husband, Larry, and I were married on a beautiful October day. It was a wonderful day but shadowed by the fact that both my mother and father had died the previous year. As I walked down the aisle, my thoughts were with them, wishing for their presence on this day my mother and I so often discussed.

On October 13, 1971, our daughter, Molly, was born. Her birth followed a miscarriage the year before, so her safe delivery into our lives filled us with joy.

As she became a young woman, I dreamed of her wedding day, praying that her father would be there to walk her down the aisle and I would be waiting for them in the front row seat. Unlike our wedding, Molly's wedding would be perfect—totally without sadness and filled with great happiness.

This was not to be. Instead, her father and I walked down the aisle holding hands, followed by sixteen of Molly's young friends escorting her casket to the front of the church.

Chapter 1

Our Story—Our Memories

Molly Marie was born October 13, 1971, at 9:24 P.M. Her grandfather, Dr. Lawrence E. Maurer, was in the delivery room along with my husband, Larry, waiting anxiously for his first grandchild to be born. Shortly after her birth, the proud grandfather gently cleaned our baby girl, wrapped her in a blanket, and proceeded to the waiting room where family members and friends were gathered. As with the birth of any child, there was great joy and pride.

We assumed Molly would not be an only child and that siblings would follow. Most parents of only children do not plan it that way, but it happens for a variety of reasons. People through the years, previous to Molly's death, asked my husband and me if we regretted having only one child. Our answer was an emphatic *no!* We were so grateful to have been blessed with this child of ours and for the joy that she brought us.

Larry was thirty years old and I was twenty-nine when we brought our infant girl home. We had our first home, our first dog, and now our first child. Larry, being the oldest of four children, was very good with feeding and diapering chores, instructing his inexperienced wife in these parenting skills.

Life was good for us. Larry taught his daughter how to swing a golf club at the early age of two as she followed him around the golf course, loving that special time with her father. My game is tennis, so Molly held her first racquet around the age of three. We spent many hours in our driveway before graduating to the tennis courts.

Larry and his brother, Chris, decided Molly should learn to snow ski at the age of five. Though she excelled in most sports, skiing became, through the years, her favorite athletic activity.

Because Larry and I have always been very active and interested in sports, there were few outside activities we did not teach our child—from bowling and ice skating to water skiing and fishing. Our life was filled with love and companionship and, more importantly, with time shared together.

Having an only child allowed us to travel extensively with Molly. Our most memorable times were spent at a nearby lake, boating and fishing. Molly and her friends loved the long weekend trips, eating on the boat and camping on the beach.

Through the years, her friends became part of our family and our home was usually the gathering place for activities. During the high school years, many of Molly's friends gathered at our home before the school dances so that she could style their hair and help with make-up. While I was busy helping the girls, Larry would set up his camera. Our photo albums are full of wonderful pictures remembering these exciting and precious times.

During Molly's senior year in high school, Larry and I were approached by Molly and her friends to chaperone their Senior Trip to Mazatlan, Mexico. We were honored—but also frightened by the responsibility of traveling with thirty students. After many meetings with the other parents and travel agency representatives, we agreed to accompany them. The trip was filled with sunshine, beaches, and a couple of anxious moments, but we enjoyed it as much as Molly and her friends.

Christmas was our favorite time of the year, as for many years we hosted a party on Christmas Eve for our friends and their children. In the early years, Santa Claus would appear and sometimes a hayride would follow. Each year, the older children would organize a choir and hold practices at our home.

Though we were a close family, Molly was very independent and chose to attend the Arizona State University in Tempe, Arizona. When we visited the campus, she fell in love with Tempe because it reminded her of our own college town of Boulder, Colorado. Because she was not a good student, we were concerned about the size of the college, but we also were excited because family friends lived nearby in Scottsdale. We felt confident and secure knowing they could help her if any problems should arise. They proved to be of great support for her and provided a friendly home when she needed to escape dorm life.

In August of 1990, Molly and I drove to Tempe in a car loaded with clothes, CDs, a tennis racquet, and photo albums filled with pictures of her many friends she was leaving behind. That special week we spent together meeting roommates, registering for classes, and decorating her room, will always be one of my most favorite memories of Molly—and one of my last.

In October, Molly's 19th birthday fell over Parents Weekend at Arizona State. We were thrilled! Of the three of us, I'm not sure who was the most excited about the weekend. Molly told us on the telephone that her friends did not understand why she was so happy about our visit. She told them we were her best friends! How dear those words are to us now. The weekend was wonderful—shopping, meeting her new friends, and taking a few of them to dinner in celebration of her birthday.

On our anniversary in late October, Molly called to say our present would be arriving in the evening and to please stay home. When the doorbell rang, we had no idea what to expect. Two of her friends stood before us with twenty or so balloons—and behind the balloons stood Molly. What a great surprise for our anniversary!

She flew home for Thanksgiving weekend and drove home with a friend for Christmas break. After our traditional Christmas Eve party and Christmas day festivities, the three of us joined other friends traveling to the Orange Bowl to watch Colorado University and Notre Dame. The week spent in Ft. Lauderdale, Florida, holds special memories for us. The entire Christmas holiday was filled with wonderful moments together sharing, laughing, and loving. Little did we know it would be our last Christmas together.

In February, Larry was to attend a convention being held in Las Vegas, Nevada. Because Tempe, Arizona, is so close to Las Vegas, we sent Molly an airline ticket to join us for the weekend. We spent hours shopping, talking over long dinners, and attending Larry's business functions. You could see and even feel the pride in Larry's heart as he introduced Molly to his various business associates and friends.

My eyes at this moment are filled with tears as I remember saying goodbye to my beautiful daughter—for it was the last time her father and I were to see her alive.

My Photo Album

The photo album of my mind
Holds treasured thoughts of you,
And I can almost see again
The things we used to do.
    I hear your voice; I see your smile;
I feel you close to me.
The photo album of my mind
Shows how we used to be.
    Time may have changed us through the years,
But I will always find
You're just as I remember in
The album of my mind.
    And, as I turn page after page,
Such precious scenes I see.
The photo album of my mind
Is very dear to me.
    It holds the pictures of our past
Like reels of film unwind.
I cherish all those photos in
The album of my mind

Jeanne Losey
Shelbyville, Indiana

Chapter 2

The Shock of Death

Larry and I had just returned from lunch and the phone was ringing as we entered the back door. It was March 17, 1991—St. Patrick's Day.

Larry ran to the kitchen telephone to grab it before the message machine activated. As I casually entered the kitchen, I noticed that his face was very pale—almost white in color. I knew something was terribly wrong and somehow knew it was about Molly. My exact words to him were "Is it about Molly?" As he shook his head yes, I asked "Is she dead?" His reply was "Maybe." My heart started pounding as I felt hysteria building inside of me.

The phone call was from the father of one of Molly's friends traveling with her to Mazatlan, Mexico, for spring break vacation.

Molly and three of her close friends from Arizona State University had decided to take a train from Nogales, Mexico, to Mazatlan for spring holiday. She had a part-time job and was paying for the trip from her earnings. Their plans were made through a travel agency in Phoenix. We were thrilled they were taking a train rather than driving or flying. What could be more safe? Little did we know—little did Molly know! She called us on Friday evening, March 15, 1991, to say goodbye, as she and her friends were driving from Tempe to Nogales early the next morning to catch the train. We all exchanged "I love you"s and "have a good time." She had wanted us to meet her there but Larry was scheduled for shoulder surgery that week, so it was not possible. Molly told us she would call upon her arrival in Mazatlan. She never arrived.

The parent informed us that Molly was missing and may have fallen from the train. We couldn't believe it—how does one fall from a train? He gave us the phone numbers of her friends now in Mazatlan as well as the American Consulate's office in Hermosillo, Mexico. We immediately called the girls in Mazatlan and upon hearing about the hazardous conditions of the train, knew Molly must have fallen. We were horrified but hoped she might have survived the fall. Though her friends begged the Mexicans to stop the train, they would not—nor would they allow the girls to get off at the first stop to go back and look for her. They were forced to ride another fifteen hours to Mazatlan knowing that their friend was most likely lying somewhere along the railroad tracks.

I immediately called my brother, Mike Kramer, and his wife, telling them that Molly was in trouble in Mexico and might be dead and we needed their help. Larry's parents were vacationing in Rincon, Mexico, as they did every year. He called his brother, Chris, to find out their phone number in Rincon and asked Chris to notify the rest of Larry's family here in Boulder. Fortunately, his parents were immediately found for the emergency telephone call and Larry was able to relay the story about Molly's accident.

The American Consulate's office advised us that a search for Molly was in progress. While friends and family members arrived at our home, I packed our suitcase and Larry made arrangements for us to fly to Hermosillo to aid in the search for our daughter. Our sister-in-law phoned the consulate's office to inform them of our arrival time. She was told that Molly's body had been found.

The horrible shock of that moment will stay clear in my mind for the rest of my life. The "unspeakable" had happened to us—a parent's worst nightmare—our child—our only child—was dead!

Our home was suddenly filled with tears and disbelief. There were few words spoken—just shocked and pained expressions. Larry and I stared at each other, wondering how we would survive and hating the unfairness and injustice of Molly's fate.

Larry very quickly entered a state of shock which he would not come out of for nearly a year. I, on the other hand, remembering the deaths of my mother and father and the ensuing shock, refused to enter that phase of grief. Though the state of shock is supposed to protect us from pain, I personally needed or chose to accept the pain immediately. I wanted to be alert and aware of everything that was to occur.

After shoving items off a bookcase in our family room, I retreated *without tears* to Molly's room and quietly sat on her bed holding her stuffed Christmas bear in my arms. Not until several of her friends arrived and gathered on and around the bed did I shed the first of many tears. Larry joined us there and together we wept in her room—a room that held so many fond memories for all of us—a room that would never be the same.

Among the friends that filled our house that evening, five couples had lost children—one of them just six months prior to Molly's death. I looked into each of their faces and knew that *now* I truly understood their pain and their terrible grief.

To All Parents

I'll lend you for a time a child of Mine, God said,
For you to love her while she's here and mourn for when she's dead.
It may be six or seven years, fourteen or twenty-three,
But will you til I call her back, take care of her for Me?

She'll bring her charms to gladden you and should her stay be brief
You'll have her lovely memories as a solace for your grief.
I cannot promise she will stay, since all from earth return,
But there are lessons taught below I want this child to learn.

I've looked this wide world over in search for teachers true
And from the throngs that crowd life's lanes I have selected you.
Now will you give her all the love, not think the labor vain
Nor hate me when I take this "lent" child back again.

I fancied that I heard them say, "Dear Lord, Thy will be done.
For all the joys Thy child shall bring, the risk of grief we'll run.
We'll shelter her with tenderness, we'll love her while we may
And for the happiness we've known forever grateful stay.

But should the angels call for her much sooner than we'd planned
We'll brave the bitter grief that comes and try to understand."

Edgar Guest

Chapter 3

Surviving The First Year

Molly died on a Saturday night, her body was found on Sunday, and she was returned to us on the following Tuesday evening by way of a private ambulance plane, accompanied by her grandparents and her uncle. Her funeral and burial followed on Friday.

After a week of solid activity—difficult decisions—and a house filled with friends and family, my husband and I found ourselves alone. What an experience to suddenly realize that our active, happy social world had ended—Molly was gone. Life would never be the same!

Larry returned to work but could not function adequately. I faltered around the house knowing what I should do—but couldn't. At night we would hold each other and cry, thanking God we still had one another. Many people who lose children are also single parents. It must be even more traumatic for them. I cannot relate to that situation in this book because it was not our situation, but I sincerely hope someone does in the near future. A single parent writing of his or her pain and recovery would be most helpful to other single parents.

It has been four years for Larry and me since Molly's death. How have we managed—what *tools* did we use? We have the following suggestions:

1. *Do not return to work too soon*—People will advise you to get back to your normal activities as soon as possible because it will take your mind off what has happened. However, returning too quickly provides an easy means for *denying* what has happened, and allows one to postpone facing reality. Larry returned to his job confused and disoriented, and came home at night to take care of me and my pain. His job occupied his mind as well as his time, allowing him to delay the grieving process. Ten months later—not long before the first anniversary of Molly's death—he

confessed to me and to our minister that he needed counseling. Perhaps a few more days at home after the funeral would have been beneficial.

Please do not misunderstand me. We both know that being active as soon as possible is most important for recovery, but *do* give yourself sufficient time to mourn before returning full time to a job.

2. *Be good to yourself*—If you don't *have* to do something—DON'T! In the first few weeks of grieving, do only what you feel capable of handling. Allow friends and family members to cook meals and run errands. Accept everyone's help and remember—by permitting them to help you, you are helping them. People cannot take away your pain, but they so much want to do whatever they can to make life easier for you. Don't be afraid to ask for help and be open and honest about your feelings and your pain.

3. *Protect your health*—I understand completely the feeling that you don't really care—but you must. Your heart and your mind have suffered the most severe of all blows. Try to eat balanced meals, get as much sleep as possible, and slowly begin to exercise.

4. *Communicate*—For the last decade, we've all been told the importance of communication. Now, communicating is imperative for your well-being. Share your thoughts and tears with anyone willing to listen. Discuss your feelings of sadness openly. Withholding your emotions can make you physically ill. Speak of your memories and mention your child's name without hesitation.

5. *Avoid major changes and decisions in your life*—You have been through the worst trauma of your life. It is no time to sell your house, change jobs, or move out of state. You need the support and love of all that is familiar. You must not stray from what is still concrete and stable, because you are temporarily weak, vulnerable, and extremely fragile. You will know when the time is right to make changes.

6. *Don't dispose of or give away anything belonging to your child for several weeks or months*—You may regret decisions made too quickly. More is said on this topic in Chapter 6.

7. *Holidays*—Mother's Day—Father's Day—Christmas— birthdays! How does one handle these holidays when your child is gone? Molly died in March—Easter, Mother's Day, and Father's Day soon followed. We were fortunate that Molly's friends spent Mother's Day with us and visited on Father's Day that first year. We celebrated Molly's birthday in October with several of her friends. We gathered first at the cemetery, followed by a cookout at our home. It was consoling for all of us to share memories and tears.

   The first year we chose to be away from home for Christmas and Thanksgiving. To be with either one of our families was impossible for us with Molly missing from her usual chair at the dining room table. Thanksgiving was spent in Las Vegas and Christmas on a two-week driving trip to California. More is mentioned on holidays in my previous book *I Don't Know How To Help Them*.

8. *Anniversary of your child's death*—Though all the holidays were difficult, we were the least prepared for the first anniversary of Molly's death. A bereaved parent advised us to be anywhere but home on that day. Thank God we took her advice and made plans in advance. The days previous to March 16th found us more depressed and overwhelmed with sadness than ever before.

   I tell you these facts not to discourage you but to prepare you. When the holidays seem unbearable, plan a camping trip, visit friends out of state, or simply do something you would ordinarily not be doing on those particular occasions. Go bowling—volunteer at your church to serve meals, plan a get-together with other bereaved parents—or simply cook steaks instead of your usual turkey.

9. *Accept the pain*—In the first few weeks, the pain is like a knife cutting through your heart. No one can describe it adequately—only bereaved parents know the intensity of this pain. Seven months after Molly's death, I realized fighting the pain was useless—why not accept it? It was and is *my* pain for *my* child and no one can take it from me. Once the decision was made to accept the pain, I felt a certain relief deep within myself. I was tired of fighting—now it was time to *learn* to live with the pain.

10. *Autopsy*—If your child died unexpectedly from an undetermined cause, you will, of course, want to read the autopsy. On the other hand, if your child was involved in a brutal accident where multiple injuries were obviously incurred, I would strongly advise you not to read a detailed autopsy. Molly's report was mistakenly sent to us. Reading it was an error in judgment that we now must live with and try somehow to forget as much as is possible.

11. *Tools for helping yourself*—In the beginning of this chapter, I mentioned *tools*. I'm referring to any item, group, or person that might help you through the first year. We tried everything—some helped and some didn't—but listed below are various suggestions you might want to try.

    a. *Grief books*—Go to your local bookstore or library and obtain as many books as possible. Many are written by bereaved parents. Reading helped me more than anything else.

    b. *Journals*—Buy yourself a journal and one for your spouse if you are a two-parent family. Write letters to your child or use your journal as a diary. Write of your pain, your anger, and your love. Writing can help relieve some of your stress and relate more sufficiently your emotions.

    c. *Candles*—Buy a candle and let it burn while you are having dinner—light it on special occasions—or light it any time you are feeling low. It is not a substitute for your child, but it can fill a void as the flame represents your child's spirit.

d. *Grief groups*—There are many groups willing and ready to help you either through meetings or newsletters. Many churches have bereaved parent groups and most local hospice organizations have weekly meetings. Some bereavement groups are listed in the back of this book. Groups are not for everyone, but you owe it to yourself to try them.

e. *Religious affiliations*—Clergymen from your own church or another church can help you greatly through the first year. If you are not presently associated with a particular church, ask a friend for suggestions. Though the clergyman may not have lost a child, he can pray for you and with you, and be there for support night or day when you need it the most.

f. *Grief cassettes*—These are useful while driving to work or traveling on a trip. They are especially good for those of you who have a difficult time reading or who do not have the time to read.

g. *Cemetery*—Spend as much time at your child's grave as you feel necessary. Don't be intimidated by those who suggest you are spending *too much* time there. We have a plastic bag at Molly's gravestone where friends and family can place greeting cards, letters, or mementos. There are a variety of stuffed animals and gifts at the grave. During the Christmas season, we put a wreath on the grave and family members and friends add new ornaments each year.

h. *Message machine*—If you don't have a message machine, this is an excellent time to purchase one. You can ignore the calls you don't wish to take and return the calls that are important.

In closing this chapter, I want to say to take one day at a time and be prepared for ups and downs. One day you may feel pretty good— and the next day as though you are falling apart. For a while every step you take forward, you seem to take two backwards. Don't be discouraged. You may not realize it, but each day you are getting stronger—it just does not always seem that way.

"One night I had a dream..."

I dreamt I was walking along a beach with God and across the sky flashed scenes from my life. For each scene I noticed two sets of footprints in the sand, one belonged to me and the other to God.

When the last scene of my life flashed before us, I looked back at the footprints in the sand. I noticed that at times along the path of life there was only one set of footprints. I also noticed that it happened at the very saddest times of my life. This really bothered me and I questioned God about it.

"God, you said that once I decided to follow you, you would walk with me all the way, but I noticed that during the most troublesome times in my life there is only one set of footprints. I don't understand why in times I needed you most, you would leave me."

God replied, "My precious, precious child, I love you and I would never leave you during your times of trials and suffering. When you see only one set of footprints it was then that I carried you."

Anonymous

Chapter 4

Mental and Physical Problems

After the death of a child, we are bewildered by the reactions of our body and mind. We do not seem to function normally. We are terribly confused by our own inadequacies and frightened by our irregular behavior. Are these problems normal under the circumstances? Yes! We have been deeply afflicted with pain.

Webster's Dictionary defines *affliction* as follows: "The state of being afflicted; a state of acute pain or distress of body or mind; the cause of continued pain of body or mind. Affliction is acute mental suffering caused by the loss of something cherished."

If you should experience any of the problems listed in this chapter, know that you are not alone, and that with time you will return to a more normal state.

1. **Concentration**—Discovering your limited ability to concentrate either at home or at the office is discouraging. You may have to read a chapter of a book several times before you grasp its meaning. At a social gathering you may lose the concept of a conversation. What once were routine tasks at your job might now seem beyond your talents. While performing duties of any kind, your mind may drift off in several different directions.

2. **Comprehension**—This is a scary one—learn to laugh at yourself. In the first few weeks I could not have comprehended an instruction book on how to turn on my stove, much less put together a gas grill! Don't push yourself too hard or attempt complicated projects too soon.

3. **Memory**—The phone number for my husband's office had been the same for eighteen years—after Molly's death, I found myself looking it up in the telephone book! Remembering names,

appointments, and favorite recipes was often impossible. Learn to make detailed lists of what you want to accomplish in a day's time—it helps.

4. **Emotions**—Your emotions are out of control. One moment you might be driving along in your car thinking you are having a rather good day—only to find yourself a couple of blocks down the road, fully engulfed in tears. You may be in a restaurant with friends when the tears seem to erupt from nowhere. Your emotions for a while will react erratically to any number of situations—a certain song, a newspaper article, a morning sunrise, an evening moon, a beautiful flower.

5. **Decision making**—For a while, it may take you ten times longer to make a decision on what to have for dinner, what jeans to wear, or when to walk the dog. Don't worry about it—most decisions do not have to be made immediately anyway.

6. **Apathy**—Feelings of insensitivity for others' problems and feelings of indifference for other people's needs are normal. You have all you can handle right now just getting yourself through each day. Be good to yourself now and in time you will be able to respond more normally.

7. **Sleep problems**—In the first days after the death of your child, you may require medication to help you sleep. Gradually you will want to eliminate medication because it can become addictive. Try walking or some type of exercise. Hot tubs or whirlpool baths are great methods of relaxation.

8. **Lack of energy**—Grieving is exhausting. Expect to be more tired than usual even though you may have slept well through the night.

9. **Night sweating**—Larry and I both suffered for several weeks from night-time sweating during our sleeping hours. We awakened to find our sheets and night clothes soaked with perspiration. Larry's problem eventually subsided, but I had entered menopause and required medication. Though my age was appropriate for menopause, I believe Molly's death hastened the inevitable.

10. **Eating habits**—During the week of Molly's death, friends forced me to eat and it seemed as if every bite stuck in my throat. Larry, on the other hand, ate normally and although his consumption was the same as usual, he lost weight. A bereaved parent may in time either return to normal weight or surpass it and continue gaining abnormally. Depression is a well-respected reason for weight gain, so beware and be careful. Being overweight can lead to severe health problems.

11. **Digestive problems**—Though you require food to maintain your health, it's advisable to stay away from spicy and acidic foods for a period of time. Diarrhea, ulcers, and basic stomach aches may result if you don't follow a bland diet. Wait a while for your favorite dishes or test them slowly and see how you handle them.

12. **Sexual problems**—Most bereaved parents will not have the desire or the energy for quite some time. Be patient with one another.

13. **Social activity**—Large parties and cocktail talk may not appeal to you right now. Try dinner with a small group of friends. Celebrations of any kind may not be part of your agenda for quite some time.

Larry and I were afraid we might not fully recover from the problems we experienced after Molly's death, but we have. Your improvement will be gradual—be patient.

Chapter 5

Difficult Situations

This chapter is to forewarn you of everyday events that may cause you unexpected pain. We were somewhat prepared for the obvious causes of sadness, but had no idea how deeply hurt we could be by the trivial matters of normal day-by-day living.

You cannot escape these situations because they are part of everyone's life, but just maybe reading about them will better prepare you for these unavoidable sources of grief.

1. **Change of seasons**—With each change of season comes a different memory of previous events, and the realization that your child will not be experiencing that season with you.

2. **The gravestone**—Seeing for the first time your child's gravestone in place is traumatic. I was overwhelmed, for it was another verification that my child had died. For most people, however, this will pass and the gravesite will be a place of contentment and peace—a place where you can talk with your child and take cards and gifts expressing your love.

3. **Phone calls and mail**—I assumed everyone must know about Molly's death, but it wasn't so. If your child was a young adult when he or she died, you may still receive mail or telephone calls for them.

4. **Graduations**—Knowing your deceased child's peers are graduating from middle school, high school, or college, without your child among them is a very sad and painful experience.

5. **TV or radio commercials**—The clever and often charming advertisements we hear around holidays such as Christmas, Father's Day, Mother's Day, and Thanksgiving, will be difficult because they are geared toward the interaction of families. Year round there are ads involving parent and child, promoting various products such as cereals and restaurants. The first year or

two after the death of your child, these advertisements may be most upsetting—turn them off!

6. **Card shops**—A couple of months after Molly's death, I stopped by a card shop for a birthday card for a friend, not realizing that Mother's Day was very near. The enormous display of Mother's Day cards forced me from the store immediately.

7. **Grocery stores**—This may seem ridiculous, but your first few shopping sprees may be stressful for you. Just seeing my daughter's favorite foods brought back memories—Pop Tarts™ for a quick breakfast before the school bus arrived, her favorite ice cream for a hot summer night, and the cake mix we used to bake her favorite dessert.

8. **Returning to a favorite vacation area**—If you shared a particular vacation spot with your child for a number of years, it may be hard to return. We have yet to return to Hawaii, but I'm sure someday we will choose to do so.

9. **Sports mutually enjoyed**—As previously mentioned, Molly and I played tennis together for many years. After her death, my first trip back to the court with friends made me feel faint and nauseated. However, I stayed with it that day and have continued to play, still loving the game as much as ever. Although Larry taught Molly the game of golf and they played often, he did not have the same immediate reaction as I. Continuing with your regular sport activities and exercise regimes is most important. On the other hand, we enjoyed boating with Molly for fifteen years, and though we tried to resume that activity at our favorite lake, it was not to be. The memories made us sad rather than happy, so after much deliberation, we made the decision to sell the boat and move on to other activities. This decision was not made in haste but rather three years after Molly's death. It was a difficult decision, but not a depressing one, for both Larry and I are looking forward to new and exciting adventures.

10. **Music**—For the first year or so, hearing one of Molly's favorite songs or those sung at her funeral caused instant tears. I learned

to listen only to talk shows on the radio while driving my car. Being temporarily blinded by tears was not safe for me or others traveling the same road.

11. **Visual resemblance of your child**—Sooner or later, and probably more than once, you will see a child resembling your deceased child. It might be on a schoolyard where children are playing, or a young adult driving a car. Not only will you temporarily be overcome by emotions, but you may find yourself staring at the individual, unable to take your eyes off him or her.

12. **Other children's deaths**—You now will be more sensitive when you read or hear of other young deaths. Not only will it renew your own grief, but you will understand the painful road ahead the newly bereaved parents must travel.

13. **Celebrations**—Joyous occasions of any kind, whether they be weddings, family get-togethers, or holiday parties, are difficult because your child is no longer with you. Attend the functions if you feel so inclined, but don't feel pressured or obligated to do so until you feel ready. If you have other children, their needs and activities will determine your social participation—more so than those of us who have lost only children.

14. **Avoidance**—Don't be surprised if some individuals seem to purposely avoid or ignore you for awhile. It does not mean they don't care or feel sympathy for you, but that they simply do not know what to say or how to handle such a delicate situation. When this happens to you, try to put yourself in their shoes and understand their awkwardness.

Now on to more delicate issues. How do you answer the question *How many children do you have?* The first time you are asked this question is monumental. Be prepared to respond. My answer to the question depends on my particular mood at that particular time. If I feel prepared to answer the hows, wheres, and whys, then my response is: I have a daughter, but she died four years ago. On other occasions, when I think it unnecessary or inappropriate to discuss it, I simply respond: I have one child. Of course, the easiest answer would be that we have no children, but that would be denying Molly's existence and that is unthinkable.

Time to move on. If you escape someone telling you this along the way, consider yourself lucky. Other friends may not be so impudent as to directly confront the issue, but you may feel their behavior indicates their feelings of impatience with your progress. Don't let comments such as these bother you. You know in your heart that you are doing the best you can. Either ignore the friends who insist you "move on" or get new friends!

Conversations with friends and family members usually revolve a great deal around children and grandchildren. Whether it be at social gatherings, the workplace, or during a golf game, most everyone enjoys discussing his or her children's activities and accomplishments. You may wonder how people can be so insensitive, but remember their lives do go forward while yours has come to a temporary stop. Only time can help you with this issue, but time does, indeed, help as the intensity of your pain decreases. Once again, this problem is more difficult for those of us who have no remaining children.

The last *difficult situation* I would like to address in this chapter concerns individuals around you complaining about what now seem to be very minor problems to those of us who have lost children. You may want to scream "You don't know what a problem is until you've walked in my shoes!" You need to remember that unless they have lost a child, they can't possibly know what you've learned. You might consider them being disadvantaged in a way, for you and I no longer allow the smaller irritations of life to bother us. The worst tragedy of all has happened to us—everything else is manageable.

Some points I've listed in this chapter no longer bother us after four years—others still do but not as much as the first year or two. Reading this chapter cannot exonerate you from the inevitable feelings you will no doubt experience, but at least you can evaluate them as normal for bereaved parents.

In summary, I might add that "realizing the world has not stopped because your child is dead" is difficult to accept, but acknowledging that fact may well be one of your first steps to recovery.

The Wind In My Arms

It's been four years
And I should be healed.
This is what I've been told.

But what do you know of my loneliness?
What do you know of my pain?
While my son is in the cemetery,
And yours just ran to the store.

While my son is in the mist
And the wind is in my arms,
And you hold yours tight
In your arms.

When you know that yours
Will come home again,
And I know mine
Never will.

JoAnn McMeans
Port Angeles, Washington

Chapter 6

Your Child's Possessions

As mentioned in Chapter 3, do not dispose of or give away anything belonging to your child for several weeks or months. There is no rush and you may regret items dispersed too soon.

After your child's death, you will want to hold, touch, and smell everything belonging to your child—clothing, dolls, jewelry, baseball bats, skis, hockey sticks, and even that favorite pair of jeans embellished with holes that previously you so wanted to discard.

These items are yours and only yours now—and only you will determine what to do with them. If family members or special friends request something specific belonging to your child, tell them you will let them know when you are ready to make decisions. You might make a list of those requests so that when and if you decide to part with certain items, you will remember who asked for them.

Most of Molly's belongings were in her college dormitory at the time of her death. Those items were carefully boxed by friends and shipped to neighbors of ours here in Boulder. Four months later, we invited Molly's closest friends to help us unpack those boxes. It was a very sad and difficult day for Larry and me—one we will never forget. However, sharing the task with Molly's friends, who so dearly loved her, helped us immensely. By that time, we had decided what things to keep and were prepared to share the rest. As each friend shared a memory about a piece of jewelry or item of clothing, we knew Molly would want that friend to have it. Though Larry and I kept some jewelry, a couple of sweaters and jackets, it felt good to give away most everything else because our daughter had always shared with her friends.

Parting with your child's possessions is very difficult and some items you may choose to keep forever. However, after some time had passed, we realized that most of the material things belonging to Molly were not that important. She is in our hearts and her spirit is very close to us. There were many individuals who wanted just a small token of her life, and many underprivileged people who could benefit from her clothing and sports equipment.

Many bereaved parents find comfort in retaining links to the past by refinishing some of the deceased child's toys and displaying them in various ways throughout their home. Another ingenious suggestion is to make a quilt or wall hanging from your child's clothing, or cut down clothing to fit a favorite stuffed animal or doll.

Larry and I sold our home and built a new house two and a half years after Molly's death. We felt a sufficient amount of time had passed and we were emotionally ready to move on. Though we were grateful to have waited that length of time, I want you to know that the packing was still most difficult. Baby dresses saved for her children, greeting cards to and from her, gifts made for us by her, which had been long forgotten, were found. There were mementos in every closet and nook of the house—tokens now lovingly and sadly remembered. The storage room and garage area produced bikes, stuffed animals, water skis, and more. With each box I packed, each item I gave away, the tears flowed and my heart ached with remembrance of past days.

On moving day, there was one last task to be performed and neither Larry nor I could do it. Molly's bedroom walls were adorned with posters, pictures, dried flowers from dances, and various other items typical of a teenager. We asked three or four of Molly's friends to remove them after we left the house. You also will find some chores are harder than others—so do ask others to help. Don't force yourself to do anything that doesn't "feel right" or is too difficult. Your friends and family want to contribute—let them.

Many of you may choose to remain in the same house after the death of your child—others simply cannot. Various circumstances will determine your decision. For Larry and me, the determining factor was the location of Molly's room. It was situated on the main level—we did not want to shut the bedroom door nor could we change the room. Therefore, relocating was the easiest solution. *We are all different—we all grieve differently and we will all take various routes to survive the deaths of our children.*

Chapter 7

Marriage

A marriage, even during the good times, can have its problems. But the odds of a marriage surviving the death of a child are frightening. I've heard various statistics such as fifty percent divorce by the first year and seventy-five percent by the fifth year. I personally have not found this to be true, but then my scope of friends and acquaintances who have deceased children is limited. I do agree, however, that losing a child is perhaps the most disruptive and challenging threat to an otherwise good marriage.

Larry and I found a whole new dimension to marriage after Molly's death. Our world had been ripped apart and we were afraid of what lay ahead of us. And though many grief books warned us of the differences in mothers' and fathers' grieving processes, we decided to survive this horrible ordeal together step by step—day by day—year after year.

This choice of commitment to one another involves six main ingredients: love, patience, understanding, communication, consideration, and compassion.

LOVE

Love is the easy one, for basically it is the accumulation of the other five ingredients. You need now to verbalize that love. A simple "I love you" to your mate at this time and throughout the grieving period is confirmation that all is not lost.

PATIENCE

Patience is one virtue few of us possess, but it is important now that each of you improve on it. Qualities that you counted on in one another may not be up to par and patience is needed to overlook those things for a while. For example, I was an extremely organized person before Molly's death—but not afterwards for a very long time. I could not remember to make grocery lists nor how to cook favorite recipes, forgot family birthdays, and neglected household chores. It was many months before I cared whether the house was clean or dirty—whether the sheets had been changed or the dry cleaning delivered or picked up.

Larry, on the other hand, who was always even-tempered, easily became irritated and provoked. His excellent qualities of promptness and perfection often failed him.

We were both plagued with acute memory loss and forgetfulness to the point of mutual laughter. Perhaps allowing ourselves to laugh at ourselves, and occasionally each other, contributed to overcoming our impatience with one another.

UNDERSTANDING

Understanding that each of you is now a different person is mind-boggling in itself. I personally believe understanding comes from knowledge—particularly in this situation. Read everything you can get your hands on—go to support groups, talk to other bereaved parents. Do everything and anything to better acquaint yourself with the situation and to familiarize yourself with the process of grieving. Only with understanding can you help one another.

COMMUNICATION

I can't say enough about communication—your thoughts and feelings must be conveyed—it is imperative. Personality traits play an immense part, for normally within a marriage, one of the two partners is more inclined to hold back, hide feelings and emotions, and be less communicative. That person must be encouraged on a daily basis to share his thoughts, discuss his fears and anxieties, and to cry openly. Tears, remember, are healing.

Ask each day how your mate is doing—though most of the time it will be apparent. Discuss the difficult moments that occurred during the past twenty-four hours. Many times one partner may have endured a rather good day and the spouse appears depressed and sullen. This is to be expected, for the ups and downs of grieving are constant. Sometimes the morose partner may need to be alone for a while, but more often than not, talking will release the emotional tension.

CONSIDERATION

Be considerate of one another in everything you do. Don't make plans without the other's consent. Some functions may be difficult for you, but not your spouse. Discuss it and decide to decline or for one spouse to go alone. Don't force activities on one another. Larry and I do not always understand completely the other's decision, but we comply without resentment.

COMPASSION

Don't believe for a minute that one of you is suffering more than the other. Each of you has been profoundly affected by the death of your child. Although we may each respond to grief in a different way, the pain of loss is the same. A hug, a gentle touch, a kiss, holding the other's hand, are gestures that say you understand and care deeply.

Following the death of a child, a marriage is fragile. Treat it as such. Being thoughtful of one another in an unselfish manner can only enhance your relationship during this difficult time.

If you are among the fortunate ones who have other children, remember they are counting on the strength, love, and security that is afforded by your marriage.

Don't be a statistic.

Chapter 8

Friends

"I didn't find my friends: the good God gave them to me."
Ralph Waldo Emerson

You cannot put a price on friendship. True friendships travel through the best of times and survive the worst of times. Most of your friends will stay by your side during your grieving period—some will not. Some will be there in the beginning and then fade away—others will come later and stay for a while or forever.

Friends you expect to be there the first few days may not appear or, if they do, their stay may be brief. Understand that some individuals cannot bear to see a friend in such agonizing pain—it is not a part of their make-up. Others may not feel their association is strong enough with you to be a part of such an intimate time. They are torn by the uncertainty of what their place is in your life at this time. Later, those particular friends may confide their reasons and want to discuss them with you. Listen and be understanding of their feelings.

Some friends may be there night and day for you throughout the first horrifying weeks and then suddenly disappear for a while. Why? They need a break from your constant and never-ending sadness, tears of rage, and devastating depression. They've neglected their own families and affairs, and need to return to a more normal existence. Since your tragedy, they've not slept or eaten well, being totally consumed by your despair. Most will return when they feel stronger and more in control.

Acquaintances who were not there for you in the beginning may suddenly surface. These people, by nature, are caring and loving persons who have a great need to share your pain and to offer their help. They may or may not stay long—but their generous acts of kindness will be much appreciated by you.

Through grief therapy groups or word of mouth, you will come into contact with other bereaved parents. If they do not contact you—contact them. You will need these people, for they can give you first hand information and relate unequivocally to your situation. They will give you love and support, advice, and, most of all, understanding of the deep, deep pain you are experiencing. These new friends may stay around only as long as needed or become lifelong pals. Most bereaved parents feel a special need or obligation to minister to those unfortunate enough to follow in their footsteps—and no one is more qualified to do so.

You may lose some friends along the way and usually for one of two reasons. One reason is their discomfort at being around the "different you"—the one that is depressed and constantly crying. They want their old *familiar friend* back—the one that is not impaired by tragedy. And they are not willing to go the distance that recovery requires.

The second reason for a friend's desertion is a judgmental attitude on their part. You are not handling your grief in the same manner they would—they would do it better! They put a time limit on your grieving and you failed to honor it. That is a friendship you can live without—let it go.

Then we have the *special friends*—those that never leave your side—those that suffer through your every tear, your every mood, your every thought. They make sure you are eating, sleeping, waking up, getting to your office, exercising, surviving. These particular friends need for you to live again, because if you do—they will! It's that simple. You are a big part of their life and they need you as much as you need them. You may find them rather irritating at times because they are the ones forcing you back to a world you may not want to be a part of right now. These are indeed the friends that "come in when the whole world has gone out," and you will love these friends for all of your days.

YOUR TEARS

I dare not ask your very all;
I only ask a part.
Bring me—when dancers leave the hall—
Your aching heart.

Give other friends your lighted face,
The laughter of the years:
I come to crave a greater grace—
Bring me your tears!

Edwin Markham

Chapter 9

The Death of An Only Child

We who have lost an only child suffer no more nor less than those bereaved parents who lose one of two children or one of five children. We have, however, lost our dreams and seemingly our future; therefore, our problems are different.

Immediately after learning of Molly's death, I remember looking at my own hands, concentrating on my jewelry—the gold ring with a single diamond that Molly and Larry gave me one Christmas, my wedding rings, and the family ring passed down to me. They were supposed to be Molly's after my death—who would inherit them now? For a long time afterwards, it was very painful to put them back on each morning.

A few weeks later, my mind concentrated on the photo albums so carefully assembled through the years—photo albums that would only be important to our only child. Who would want them now—a lifetime of baby pictures, birthdays, holidays, family vacations?

On our last airplane flight together the previous Christmas, Molly picked up a bride's magazine in one of the shops before boarding the plane. There were no marriage plans for her at the time, but she and I had a great time going through the magazine, picking out favorite dresses on each page. There would be no beautiful wedding now—no wonderful son-in-law to love—no grandchildren to cherish and spoil.

As parents of only children, I do not believe we realize, until our child is gone, that we lived our lives for that child. We invested our love, our time, our money, and our future within that one wonderful human being. Everything we were—everything we did—was for the child who is no longer here. What do we do now?

I understand your heartache—your fear of the future and the dread of going through another twenty-four hours without your child. Suicide seemed for me to be the only escape from the excruciating pain. That possibility remained with me for several months. What changed my mind? There were four significant reasons why I chose life, and they are as follows:

1. My husband would be alone with no one to share his grief. He had already lost his only child; what would he do without me?

2. Had not our families and friends been through enough?

3. Molly's friends—they were young and impressionable and not sure how to deal with their pain. They were reaching out to us for strength and reassurance that life would continue.

4. Being raised in the Catholic faith, I was fearful of not going to the same place where Molly now existed.

You will survive, but where do you go from here? Take one day at a time and move forward an inch at a time. In the beginning of grief, your heart is heavy, but as time goes on, the intensity of the pain will decrease. When you feel stronger, start making plans for the future—focus on a new dream or follow through with a forgotten ambition. Do not allow yourself to dissolve—push yourself. It's tough. You have no other children to live for now—no one to force you back into reality and routine. You are in charge of your own destiny—make it worthwhile. Your child was once your legacy—now you are his. Carry that responsibility honorably and with pride. Through you, your child lives. He or she is counting on you—don't fail.

You are still a "Mom" or "Dad." No one can strip you of that title, for it was given to you by a very special person. And that special person needs you to pray for him, love him, be strong for him, and to carry on for him in some special way. Think about what was important to your child and follow through for him. You, as his parent, know of his special dreams or goals. Perhaps those dreams or goals can become part of your life now. By doing that, your life can take on new meaning without excluding your child. You can coexist in a sense of the word.

What about holidays? There were three of you—now only two, or one if a single parent. Do you participate with your extended families as usual? Do you go on a vacation far away or perhaps to the solitude of a mountain cabin or resort? Because you are now childless, you are flexible. There are no other children depending upon you to follow through with family traditions. Do whatever feels right. Larry and I have found Thanksgiving and Christmas the most painful of holidays. We normally make plans in advance to take a trip or spend time in a family cabin in a nearby mountain town. These trips include plenty of activity, as well as quiet time to reflect, discuss, and cry if necessary. We are fortunate that both our families understand that Larry and I must handle these holidays in a manner best for us.

In past Christmases, we have given the family a candle to burn in memory of Molly, a letter to be read at the dinner table, and one year, a special book titled *With Each Remembrance* by Flavia Weedn.

As time has passed, I no longer worry about who will inherit my jewelry, and if no one wants the photo albums when we're gone, so be it. I've accepted the fact that there will be no grandchildren in my future, but there are other children to love and appreciate.

Larry and I are four years into this challenge and things are going well. We have come a long way. We have jumped a few hurdles, added more to our agenda, and followed up on a dream or two. We can laugh at a good joke, enjoy being with good friends, and participate in our favorite sports once again.

We think of our daughter every day, but we now have more days without tears than with tears. We miss her smile—her laugh—her zest for life, but we have survived. We have returned to living and are taking her with us every step of the way.

" We do not need a special day..."

We do not need a special day
To bring you to our minds.
The days we do not think of you
Are very hard to find.

Each morning when we awake,
We know that you are gone
And no one knows the heartache
As we try to carry on.

Our hearts still ache with sadness
And secret tears still flow.
What it meant to lose you
No one will ever know.

Our thoughts are always with you,
Your place no one can fill.
In life we loved you dearly,
In death we love you still.

There will always be a heartache,
And often a silent tear,
But always a precious memory
Of the days when you were here.

If tears could make a staircase,
And heartaches make a lane,
We'd walk the path to Heaven
And bring you home again.

We hold you close within our hearts,
And there you will remain,
To walk with us throughout our lives
Until we meet again.

Our family chain is broken now,
And nothing seems the same,
But as God calls us one by one,
The chain will link again.

John & Bonnie Challis, grandparents
TCF/Winnepeg
Printed with permission of The Compassionate Friends, Inc.

Chapter 10

Helping Others

To One In Sorrow

Let me come in where you are weeping, friend,
And let me take your hand.
I, who have known a sorrow such as yours,
Can understand.
Let me come in—I would be very still
Beside you in your grief;
I would not bid you cease your weeping, friend,
Tears bring relief.
Let me come in—I would only breathe a prayer,
And hold your hand,
For I have known a sorrow such as yours,
And understand.

Grace Noll Crowell

As your pain begins to subside and your mind is more clear, your thoughts may turn to helping others. Most bereaved parents feel a need, if not a calling, to be of service to others in some manner.

I knew for months that I was meant to do something worthwhile in memory of my daughter, Molly. I did not know what that might be, but knew one day it would be apparent. As predicted, I woke one morning and told my husband that I intended to write three books on bereavement. I began that afternoon as if possessed, and a year later, my first book, *I Don't Know How To Help Them*, was published. I knew nothing of the art of writing and even less about the procedures involved in publishing a book. But by the grace of God, and, I believe, Molly's assistance, I found my way of "helping others."

Your own grief will prevent you from reaching out for quite some time—maybe a year or so. You may, however, be approached sooner than expected by a friend, a neighbor, or a minister, to counsel or meet with another bereaved parent. The first time you agree to do this is very stressful, for you are uncertain of finding the right words to console.

Larry and I discussed it thoroughly before our first meeting with newly bereaved parents and agreed that our message would be one of hope and encouragement. That can be difficult when you yourselves are still experiencing so much pain, but when you see the tear-stained face of one so recently shattered, you realize how far you have really come. Having been in their fragile state not so long ago, we knew it was important that we listen, allowing them to talk of their child and his or her death, and answer their painful but honest and searching questions.

There are many ways to help others—scholarships, donations to charities, volunteer work, donation of trees or equipment to your child's school, being a Big Sister or Big Brother, involvement in your own church programs, or becoming a participant in a bereavement group or organization.

Many times in the last four years I have responded to deaths reported in the newspaper, by writing a note or letter of sympathy to the bereaved parents. Though the people are usually strangers, I have been overwhelmed with the responses. Because I also am a bereaved parent, my note is always welcomed and appreciated.

I learned through the *Alive Alone* organization that by donating $60 to the National Forest for replacement of trees lost to fires, you can receive a permanent memorial plaque engraved with your child's name. This organization is called *Penny for Pines* and may be contacted by writing to the Forest Service, 900 West Grand Avenue, Porterville, California, 93257-2035.

There are many ways of contributing in memory of your child. *And remember,* we all grieve differently and for indefinite periods of time. Only you can determine when you are ready and capable of helping others.

The Gift

I have a gift.
I did not want this gift;
It meant suffering and pain.
The pain came because of a love,
A love that had manifested itself in a child.

The child brought his love to me
And asked for my love.
Sometimes, I did not understand this.
Sometimes, I did not appreciate it.
Sometimes, I was too busy
To listen quietly to this love.
But the love persisted; it was always there.

One day the child died.
The love remained.
This time the love came in other forms.
This time there were memories,
There was sadness and anguish,
And unbelievable pain.

One day a stranger came and stood with me.
The stranger listened and occasionally spoke.
The stranger said, "I understand," and he did.
The stranger had also been this way.

We talked and cried together.
The stranger touched me to comfort.
The stranger became my friend as no other had.
My friend said "I am always here," and was.
One day I lifted my head.
I noticed another grieving,
Grey and drawn with pain.
I approached and spoke.

I touched and comforted.
I said, "I will walk with you,"
And I did.
I also had the gift.

Joe Lawley
Nuneaton, England

Chapter 11

Closure

What is closure? The *Webster Encyclopedic Dictionary* defines closure as: "The act of closing; an end or conclusion." The same dictionary defines conclusion as: "The end, close, or termination; the last part."

I want this thing called "closure" but am not sure what it is. Our friends and acquaintances have mentioned frequently that we might attain closure when the lawsuit concerning Molly's death is settled. Because the lawsuit is possibly nearing the end now, I am more curious than ever about closure and have begun to dwell upon it.

When we reach this "closure," does it mean our minds will forget or our hearts will no longer ache? I think not. Could it mean we will no longer think about what might have been if our child had lived? Of course not!

As I mentioned earlier, Larry and I are involved in a lawsuit concerning Molly's death. Horrifying negligence by the travel agency, as well as the Mexican train, prompted her death. Shortly after the funeral, we were informed that three other students had died previous to Molly and in the same manner. After four years, we have little faith left in the justice system. However, we have, through our attorneys, accomplished two important achievements. The travel agency has not used the Mexican train for transporting students to and from Mexico since we originally initiated our lawsuit. By way of settlement, we hope also to have the travel agency sign a document stating that it will not resume using the train in future years. Our second accomplishment, once again through our attorneys, is that all travel agents now must warn their clients of all possible dangers and past fatalities associated with any trips or tours.

If there is a lawsuit such as ours, a settlement or court trial would mean an end to that segment of grieving, and, reasonably, another step toward closure is obtained.

Larry and I are also planning a trip to Mexico to place a cross at the location where Molly's body was found. I believe "closure" for us can only be acquired when this final but painful duty is performed.

When a child dies a "sudden death" and there is no time to say goodbye—no time for a last hug or "I love you," you are left feeling not only robbed but in a state of disbelief. *Acceptance* comes more slowly because you were not there to witness this death that happened so suddenly and without warning.

If your child is murdered, closure is not possible until the murderer is tried and convicted. That makes sense to me. That episode of your child's death can now be *terminated*, and you may proceed with the healing process. What if the murderer is not caught—can closure occur?

What if a child takes his own life? I can only try to understand that kind of heartache for the surviving parent or parents. I'm aware that there are many organizations and support groups for the survivors of suicide. From my understanding, self-imposed guilt must be dealt with before any peace of mind can be obtained by the survivors. Does "closure" then follow?

If your child dies from a lingering illness, when does closure begin? Does it begin with the acceptance of the illness, the conclusion of life, or when the "after death" duties are performed?

Sudden Infant Death Syndrome. What a shock to find your supposedly healthy baby dead in his crib! There is no preparation possible for this type of death. Is closure possible?

Stillborns. You have loved this child since inception. Your dreams had begun for his or her future. Now you have delivered a child who will never know life. Stillborn deaths receive the least amount of sympathy down the road because friends and family members do not understand such severe grief for a chid who never lived. They cannot comprehend the love you had already invested in the child for nine months. Closure must be most difficult.

I am not sure why the word "closure" is so intriguing to me, but I would assume because of its common usage in today's society. The word is not only associated with death, but with other situations as well. I am not sure, as an individual, whether "closure" can or does take place after the death of a child.

However, I have drawn some "uncertain" conclusions on this matter:

1. Perhaps closure means a certain amount of peace has been obtained when *acceptance* of a child's death occurs. After four years, I now accept the fact that Molly will not be returning and that our lives must go on without her.

2. Closure may be what is denied us as bereaved parents until all loose ends are tied together, all questions answered, and all "after death" duties completed.

3. Closure does not mean an end to grieving, but rather provides us with an unobstructed path to move on to the final phase of grieving.

I would like to add here that my belief is that the "final phase" of grieving is what we, as bereaved parents, experience for the rest of our lives. In other words, grieving does not end, but does indeed become manageable.

Recently an article appeared in our local newspaper, *The Daily Camera*, concerning the fusillade at Kent State, May 4, 1970. A mother of one of the slain victims stated, "I'm leading a normal life and I behave very well," and added that she is going back to Kent State, hoping "there will be some kind of closure for me."

Perhaps my next book will be devoted entirely to "closure." Write to me at the address listed in the front of this book and let me know what *your* views are on closure. Your letters may be the substance of the book. Please include a permission for reprint.

Chapter 12

The Spiritual World and Dreams

As previously mentioned, I was raised in the Catholic faith and though I had not been a "practicing Catholic" for some years, my faith in God was strong—until Molly was killed. After her death, there could be no "God," for, if one did exist, he would not have taken my only child from me. I was not angry at God because, in my mind, there was *no* God.

I would like to tell you now what events in my life brought me back—back not only to God but to a belief in the spiritual world.

On a Sunday afternoon, two weeks to the day we were informed of Molly's death, Larry and I were depressed *literally* beyond words. Until that day, we had managed to comfort one another with words, hugs, and a sufficient amount of understanding. But on this particular day, we could not help one another—we could barely talk or have any sort of conversation. That afternoon, Larry fell asleep on one of the couches in the family room. I was so terribly depressed that I did not believe I could make it through another twenty-four hours. I was suicidal and knew it. I lay down on the other couch, tossing and turning, praying for some kind of peace—at least enough peace to obtain a couple hours of sleep.

Suddenly I felt a presence behind me and ever so gently this presence placed his hands on my shoulders. My first thought was that Molly had come back—and if I moved she would go away. I closed my eyes and sleep came quickly. I awoke three hours later, rested, refreshed, and stronger.

That evening I concentrated on this strange happening and realized it could not have been Molly, for the presence I felt standing behind me was tall and the hands placed on my shoulders were large and comforting. Molly was neither tall nor of a large build. It was then the realization came to me—God knew I was on the edge and He answered my prayer.

Three weeks after Molly's death, her friends at Arizona State University planned a memorial for Molly at the campus church in Tempe, Arizona. One of Molly's young friends from Colorado, who had missed her funeral in Boulder, decided to drive to Tempe for the memorial. Because of a snow storm, he pulled into a truck stop and determined that he could not go on in his late model car. His decision was to wait for a truck with Arizona license plates that might permit him a ride to Arizona. Within a short time, a brand new rig pulled into the truck stop with Arizona license plates. The young man was granted his wish to ride along and he conversed with the driver about Molly and her tragic death. The truck driver was a counselor for young people at his church in Arizona and was able to help Molly's young friend with his pain and grief. Not only did the wonderful man deliver this friend to Arizona, but he also dropped him off in Tempe at Molly's dorm where her friends were waiting for him. Coincidence—perhaps—but you will never convince Molly's friend that it was.

Several months later, I found myself once again wracked with pain, and returned to my bedroom in the middle of the day. I had no will power nor the strength to continue on that day. As I lay on my bed, sobbing uncontrollably, I heard Molly say, "Mom, you are not even trying!" Though I could not see her, I felt her presence at the end of the bed. With anger, I sat up and shouted, "Molly, I am too trying!" As I sat there alone in my bedroom, my thoughts were: I have really lost it now! But you know, after composing myself, I returned to my household duties and accomplished more that day than I had in several weeks.

Then there are *dreams*. I'm not an expert on dreams by any means, but I do believe they are a tool to help us in some situations. Unfortunately, not everyone dreams of his or her deceased child—

Larry has had only one and myself maybe three or four. One of those dreams allowed me to see Molly *not* as a teenager, but as a young woman. Her hair was shorter and she told me about her life as it is now. She informed me about the college courses she was taking and how well she was doing. School was difficult for Molly because of some slight learning disabilities. I felt great relief knowing she was not having those same difficulties in her new existence. But more importantly, I awoke feeling she was no longer stuck in time and was indeed maturing at the same pace as her friends here on earth.

The purpose of this chapter is to suggest you keep an open mind and open heart. Don't be so bitter or distraught that your child finds it impossible to connect with you in some way.

When disasters happen, such as the bombing in Oklahoma City, I once again doubt the existence of God, but then I remember my personal experiences since Molly's death and reconsider. God is not the reason bad things happen—human beings cause most disasters and meaningless deaths. God is saddened by all tragedies. He feels our pain and cries with us and, if we allow it, He will help us through our individual traumas and heartaches.

In closing, I do not believe our children leave us by dying, for the bond and love between a parent and child is too strong. For that reason, though you can no longer see your child in the physical form, I feel "your child is standing beside you."

" *Death is nothing at all.* "

Death is nothing at all. I have only slipped away into the next room. I am I, and you are you, and the old life that we lived so fondly together is untouched, unchanged. Whatever we were to each other, that we are still. Call me by the old familiar name. Speak of me in the easy way which you always used. Put no difference into your tone. Wear no forced air of solemnity or sorrow. Laugh as we always laughed at the little jokes that we enjoyed together. Play, smile, think of me, pray for me. Let my name be ever the household word that it always was. Let it be spoken without an effort, without the ghost of a shadow upon it. Life means all that it ever meant. It is the same as it ever was. There is absolute and unbroken continuity. Why should I be out of mind because I am out of sight? I am but waiting for you, for an interval, somewhere very near, just round the corner. All is well.

Henry Scott Holland (1847-1918)

Chapter 13

In Conclusion

Larry and I have come a long way since that dreadful Sunday four years ago. The good days now outnumber the bad. We are not the *same* people we once were, but we are indeed more compassionate, sympathetic, and understanding of other people's needs and sorrows.

We have returned to living and to life as we knew it before Molly's death. There have been changes and probably more to come, but we are satisfied with our progress. We ignore those who judge us and appreciate those who give us their continued support and love.

Though the pain will never completely leave us, we have indeed learned to live with it. We miss our beloved Molly every day and know that a part of us is forever gone, but we can now appreciate a beautiful day, and laughter is once again a part of our lives.

My thoughts and prayers are with you as you begin your journey through the grieving process. Take your time—be patient—and remember that your child is very near, watching over you with loving care.

God bless each and every one of you.

Appendix A:
Bereavement Groups

Alive Alone, Inc.
11115 Dull Robinson Road
Van Wert, OH 45891

Literature distributed by *Alive Alone, Inc.*, describes itself as "a non-profit corporation organized for such educational and charitable purposes as will benefit bereaved parents whose only child or all children are deceased, by providing a self-help network and publications to promote communication and healing, to assist in resolving their grief, and a means to reinvest their lives for a positive future."

American Self-Help Clearinghouse
201-625-7101

For listings and directories in finding or forming mutual aid self-help group.

Association for Death Education and Counseling (ADEC)
638 Prospect Avenue
Hartford, CT 06105-4298

Bereavement Magazine
8133 Telegraph Drive
Colorado Springs, CO 80920

A magazine of hope and healing.

Bereavement Support Group Program for Children
Participant Workbook and Leader Manual
Accelerated Development, Inc., Publishers
3400 Kilgore Avenue
Muncie, IN 47304-4896
317-284-4896

Bereavement Support Program
Caledonia Home Health Care
PO Box 383 St. Johnsbury, VT 05819
802-748-8116

Learning about grief—a guide to group discussions with children.

Camp Hope Helping Others Pain End
816 2nd Street N Steens Point, WI 54481
715-341-0076

A camp for grieving children.

Center for Loss and Grief Therapy
Linda Goldman, MS
Co-Director Ellen Zinner, PsyD
10400 Connecticut Avenue, Suite 514
Kensington, MD 20895-3944
301-942-6440

Provides counseling and support services for grieving adults, children, and perinatal loss.

Center for Loss and Life Transition
Dr. Alan Wolfelt
3735 Broken Bow Road
Ft. Collins, CO 80526
303-226-6050

Center for Loss in Multiple Birth (Climb, Inc.)
Jeane Kollantai
PO Box 1064
Palmer, AK 99645

Support group by and for parents who have experienced the death of one, both, or all of their children during a twin or higher multiple pregnancy, at birth or in infancy.
Includes parents who have undergone selective reduction as well as parents who have learned that one twin has serious anomalies.
Wonderful resource organization for parents.

Centering Corporation
1531 North Saddle Creek Road
Omaha, Nebraska 68104-5064
402-553-1200

Bereavement Publishing Company. Write or call for catalog.

Children and Grief Hospice of North Carolina, Inc.
1046 Washington Street Raleigh, NC 27605

Lesson plans included for all ages.

The Compassionate Friends
P. O. Box 3696
Oak Brook, IL 60522-3696

The *Compassionate Friends'* newsletter states that this group is a "mutual assistance self-help organization offering friendship and understanding to bereaved parents and siblings. The primary purpose is to assist them in the positive resolution of the grief experienced upon the death of a child and to support their efforts to achieve physical and emotional health."

Education Programs Associates
Customer Service
1 W Campbell Avenue, Bldg. D, Room 40
Campbell, CA 95008
617-232-8390

Good Grief: Helping groups of children when a friend dies.
Sandra Sutherland Fox
ACSW Judge Baker Children's Center
295 Longwood Avenue Boston, MA 02115
617-232-8390

Ms. Fox includes several books that provide a comprehensive view of providing services for grieving children which includes information for schools and individuals. Includes cultural and ethnic differences. She has developed and includes an extensive bibliography in her books.

Grief Counseling and Support Center of Hospice of
Winston-Salem/Forsyth County, Inc.
1100-C South Stratford Road, Suite 201
Winston-Salem, NC 27103
919-768-3972
FAX 919-659-0461

Support groups and counseling.

H.A.N.D. (Helping After Neonatal Death)
PO Box 341 Los Gatos, CA 95031
408-732-3228

Resource network for information concerning pregnancy loss and neonatal death. Resource library, phone support, peer support groups, inservice programs, newsletter.

Heartbeat
2956 S. Wolff Street
Denver, CO 80236
303-934-8464

Self-help support group for survivors of suicide. Facilitors are not professional, but all survivors.

Hope for Bereaved, Inc. Support Groups and Services
4500 Onodaga Boulevard
Syracuse, NY 13219
315-475-9675

Support groups and services, listening, counseling, and referrals. Also, telephone helpline: 315-475-HOPE (4673) These two publications are available through them: *Hope for Bereaved: Understanding, Coping and Growing Through Grief; How to Form Support Groups and Services for Grieving People.*

Human Services Press
PO Box 2423 Springfield, IL 62705
217-258-1756

Books, audio cassettes (self-help).

IN LOVING MEMORY
1416 Green Run Lane
Reston, Virginia 22090
703-435-0608

Dedicated to helping parents cope with the death of their only child or all children.

Kinder Mourn
515 Fenton Place Charlotte, NC 28207
704-376-2580

The purpose of Kinder Mourn is to assist professionals in working with bereaved families and educating the community regarding parental and sibling grief.

LARGO
1192 S. Uvald Street
Aurora, Colorado 80012
Largo is a quarterly newsletter for parents who have had more than one child die.

Minnesota Sudden Infant Death Center
Minneapolis Children's Medical Center
2525 Chicago Avenue South
Minneapolis, MN 55404
612-0863-6285

National Hospice Organization
1901 North Moore Street
Suite 901
Arlington, VA 2220

National Self-Help Clearinghouse
212-642-2944

For listings and directories in finding or forming a mutual self-help group.

Parents of Murdered Children
National Headquarters
100 E. 8th Street
Cincinnati, OH 45202 (513-721-5683)
Colorado State Coordinator: 303-722-6004

Penny for Pines
National Forest Service
900 West Grand Avenue
Porterville, CA 93257-2035

For donating $60 to the National Forest Service for tree replacement, you will receive a memorial plaque engraved with your child's name.

Pen-Parents
PO Box 8738
Reno, NV 89507-8738

Pen-Parents is a support network which provides an opportunity for bereaved parents to talk about their loss through correspondence with others in similar situations. Good resource for parents who have interrupted pregnancies.

Pregnancy and Infant Loss Center
1421 East Wayzata Boulevard
Suite 40
Wayzata, MN 55391

Non-profit organization offering support, resources, and education on miscarriage, stillbirth, and infant death.

SHARE Pregnancy and Infant Loss Support, Inc.
National SHARE Office
St. Joseph Health Center
300 First Capitol Drive St.
Charles, Missouri 63301-2893
314-947-6164
FAX 314-947-7486

The mission of SHARE is to serve those who are touched by the tragic death of a baby through miscarriage, stillbirth, or newborn death.

Appendix B: Living Through Grief

In April of 1995, an article written by Marcia Lattanzi-Licht appeared in our Boulder newspaper, The Daily Camera. *Because it was so well written and in total conjunction with my feelings expressed in this book, I asked Marcia for permission to reprint an edited version of the article. Marcia's only daughter, Ellen, was killed by a drunken driver in March of 1985. Though I did not know the Lattanzi family at the time of the incident, I remember feeling great sorrow for the families of the girls killed. My daughter, Molly, was thirteen at the time of Ellen's death.*

Marcia Lattanzi-Licht was a co-founder of Boulder County Hospice and teaches and lectures nationally on topics that include loss and professional stress. She maintained a psychotherapy practice for ten years in Boulder, Colorado, where she has resided since 1974.

One of the precious secrets that the death of someone we love brings to us is that time is our most valuable resource, and how we spend it matters a great deal. After experiencing a great loss in our own lives, there is a need to speak of the central truths of human life. We know that time and people we love are really all that matter.

Ten years ago, 1985, my oldest child and only daughter, Ellen Lattanzi, was killed by a drunken driver who ran a red light. Any parent who has lost a child knows that one of the great difficulties is continuing on into a vague unimagined future. The wish is that we could have traded our lives for those of our children. We just weren't given that choice.

The time of acute grief often feels like a nightmare, something so terrible it could not be real, and there is an intense wish to awaken and find the horrible reality was only a dream.

When the death is traumatic and violent, the nightmare of grief never goes away totally. It lingers, with lessened horror, into the remainder of our days with images that can revisit and intrude upon us. It is a nightmare that can never be completely forgotten, only lived with in ways that allow us to continue engaging with life.

Pain makes us feel a great distance and detachment from others. We long for and fear closeness, with an awareness of what else can be lost.

There is a great deal of discussion, myth, and misconception about the time needed to grieve. In our fast-paced overly pressured world, we look for easy cures, or quick ways to push legitimate sorrow aside. Corporate America gives us 3 to 5 days to deal with the deaths of people we loved the most.

Just as we believe that people heal quickly, we assume that "time heals all wounds." While time does soften the pain, it is not the only element needed to integrate a loss. The difficult work of redefining our lives takes energy, strength, support, and some measure of faith and commitment to engaging with life again.

In the early weeks of grief, there are many moments when we can rise above the pain, or briefly put it in the background. Likewise, there are also moments years later, throughout our lifetimes, when the sorrow will visit again. It doesn't have the same overwhelming power that it does initially, and is more easily taken and put in perspective.

The one part of grief that remains across time is missing the person you loved. I still have moments of longing to be with Ellen, to talk, laugh, remember, disagree, shop, cook, or just to be together. I miss the years we didn't have together, her career, wedding, grandchildren, and most of all, the ordinary family times.

Grief brings an altered sense of time, where past, present, and future mix together and co-exist with each other. Eventually, they separate out and the memories and images and experiences of the past become connections to a valued part of our lives.

There is a blessing that time holds, and that is that we are continuously called to engage with life, to love the people who are here with us. That does not mean we forget the people we love who have died. Rather, our lives represent all the people whose love has shaped us, those who are living and those who are dead.

Does grief end? The human being is not built for sustained pain or distress. We make adaptations and changes that allow us to continue on. One thing is clear. Even though someone dies, the love we feel for that person doesn't die. No amount of time can alter that. That love continues on inside us, like a song that plays on, quietly, in the background of our days.

About the author

Linda grew up in Indianapolis, Indiana, and graduated from Stephens College in Columbia, Missouri, in 1962.

She and her husband, Larry, reside in Boulder, Colorado.

She is the author of the book *I Don't Know How To Help Them*, published in 1993, after the death of her only child, Molly.